D1066274

Trails
and Turnpikes

carl e. price

illustrations by william loechel

Trails
and Turnpikes

Abingdon Press ⊕ nashville and new york

to my grandfather
SAMUEL WILEY PRICE
an oak of a man

PREFACE   This book is a selection of meditations that have come out of experiences in the out-of-doors, most of them arising from incidents on trail camps with youths from Methodist churches in New Jersey and Michigan over the past six years. Some go back further than that to experiences in scouting, to camping trips with my family, to life with my grandparents, and to hunting trips with friends and relatives. It is impossible to write acknowledgment for debts such as these, for the list of those to whom I am indebted is too long, and the interest that has accrued is too great.

It is my prayer and earnest hope that at least two things may be accomplished through this book. First, that the reader may come to a greater awareness of the wonders, the beauty, and the quiet strength that lie beyond our asphalt jungles and our stone canyons.

Secondly, and more important than the first, there is the hope that God may speak to us through these experiences in the out-of-doors. These meditations are not written to glorify nature, but to attempt to let God speak to us by our becoming sensitive to his world.

My hope is best expressed in the words of the following "Prayer of a Camper":

God of the hills, grant us thy strength to go back into the cities without faltering, strength to do our daily task without tiring and with enthusiasm, strength to help our neighbors who have no hills to remember.

God of the lake, grant us thy peace and thy restfulness, peace to bring into a world of hurry and confusion, restfulness to carry to the tired whom we shall meet every day, content to do small things with a freedom from littleness, self-control for the unexpected emergency and patience for the wearisome task, with deep depths within our souls to bear us through the crowded places. Grant us the hush of the nighttime when the pine trees are dark against the sky line, the humbleness of the hills who in their mightiness know it not, and the laughter of the sunny waves to brighten the cheerless spots of a long winter. . . .

God of the wilderness, with thy pure winds from the northland blow away our pettiness; with the harsher winds of winter drive away our selfishness and hypocrisy; fill us with the breadth and the depth and the height of thy wilderness. May we live out the truths which thou hast taught us, in every thought and word and deed. Amen.

Specific acknowledgment must be made to several who made this work possible: Mr. William Loechel, who encouraged me to put some thoughts on paper and most generously and ably contributed the drawings which reflect so well many of the moods and experiences out of which the writing came; Mrs. Nell Stoyer, who gave freely of her time to type the manuscript, including the deciphering of my notes and marginal additions; and to my wife Pat, who gave her critical ear to listen first to the spoken form and her helpful eye to the correcting of the written version.

CARL E. PRICE

CONTENTS

And he said to them, "Come away by yourselves to a lonely place, and rest a while." For many were coming and going, and they had no leisure even to eat.

Mark 6:31

TRAILS and TURNPIKES

For several summers I have spent a week or more with a group of youth hiking the trails of our state and national parks. We travel six or seven hundred miles by automobile in about a day and a half, then spend six days hiking about fifty miles. While the highways we travel take us through beautiful parts of our country, the youth are invariably more impressed with the trails than the turnpikes.

I find this quite a contrast to much of the prevailing philosophy of our day where all the premium seems to be placed on maximum speed and maximum distance in minimum time. Everything must be instantaneous, from instant breakfast to instant achievement. Our motto seems to be, "Never walk if you can run, never run if you can ride, and never ride if you can fly." Brevity is becoming an increasingly deciding factor in our economy.

Perhaps it is because time is money and money is our God; but I think it is more than this. I have a feeling that we are dealing with something much deeper than that. We have lost our feeling for eternity, and so we try to compensate by cramming as much as possible into the NOW.

Of course, the great appeal of the turnpike is its saving in time. Every trip we take to my home state of West Virginia from our present home in Michigan is accomplished in a little less time than the previous one, as new sections of interstate highways are opened up. However, as I look at the devastation of natural resources, the usurping of homes and choice land for throughway construction, and the growing ribbons of concrete and steel, I sometimes feel we are rapidly approaching the place where we will have wonderful ways of getting places, but no place to go.

When the original West Virginia turnpike was built some years ago, it started several miles outside the city of Charleston and led some sixty miles south, ending several miles from any other major city. It was often referred to as the Highway from Nowhere to No Place. This is the trouble with many of life's turnpikes. They get you where you are going fast; but—is where they lead worth going to?

I marvel at many people's idea of a vacation. It seems to be to put as many miles on the car as possible and see as many different sights as one can see in as many different parts of the country as one can get to within the allotted time. Personally, I find that sort of vacation abhorrent and not at all recreative. I don't object to going many miles to see something, but when I get there I want really to see it, feel its pulses, hear its voices, catch its spirit. It is when I take time to do this that I feel the most recreated; it is then that I can feel the wheels of life slowing down and new strength flowing in.

Our family has found one site in the hills of New Hampshire that has called us back again and again. It has a familiar look and feel about it now. We know the sound of the stream that flows a few feet from our tent; we know the song of the wind in the pine trees above us; we know the friendly smile of the sun on the mountains that tower over us and the frown of the storm clouds that can move in so quickly. It is familiar to us; and yet, it is ever new. There are new trails to walk, a different mountain to climb, the newness of the interests of the children this year as compared to two years ago, new discoveries about one another as persons.

At this rate it will take a long time to see this nation of ours, but I am convinced that I could travel a lot farther and see a lot less. Sometime or other, and hopefully sooner than later, we learn that there is more to be done with time than hurry.

Seek first his kingdom and his righteousness, and all these things shall be yours as well.
Matthew 6:33

the LUGGAGE of LIFE

It made my back ache just to look at the packs the two ladies were carrying. After four days on the trail, with a couple of rest days thrown in, we were used to walking trails instead of sidewalks, and we were adjusted to carrying packs instead of suitcases. The ladies did not appear to be so well adjusted. They came from the opposite direction, which meant the longest hike of the journey had been their first one; furthermore, their packs were bulky and poorly fitted, most ill-suited to such terrain. They were even carrying some of their equipment in their arms. That may be all right from the grocery store home or from the car to the terminal, but it is no way to go in the wilderness.

I thought of the many kinds of luggage I had seen people carrying in my lifetime. I remembered the "A" frames of the laborers in Korea; the packboards laden down with water and rations of the coolie trains that supplied our forces in the mountain; the GI pack with its customary horseshoe blanket roll across the top; the mother with the baby on her hip, carried side-saddle with a piece of cloth; the awkward, deadly burden of the machine gunner; the familiar double-arm load of the porter at the railroad station; the wide variety of packs that showed up in our trail hikes; the little child that insists on dragging about old pocketbooks and chairs and toys too big for him to carry. Man must be made for bearing burdens. The trick is deciding which ones to carry.

I remember hearing the wartime story of a traveler in the Orient who had stopped in a little village several miles from the hostilities. He was awakened in the night by a hurried call from his host who told him that the village was about to be overrun. He would not have time to pack his belongings but could take only whatever he could throw into a small suitcase. In thinking about the experience later he wrote, "What do you put into a small suitcase when you are standing on the brink of eternity?" Most of us never get down to such a vivid necessity for decision making. We travel with moving vans instead of suitcases; and that is true not only of possessions, but of activities and interests and attitudes—a change for all occasions.

On the trail one soon pares down the necessities. I have seen marines in the mountains of Korea carry half a bar of soap instead of a whole one and use it for shaving as well as washing. I have seen them tear a towel in half to lighten their pack a little more. There is only so much room in a pack; and you learn rather quickly on the trail that it is meant to carry things *inside*, not dangling all over the outside like ornaments on a Christmas tree, catching on brush and rocks and throwing the hiker off balance.

Sooner or later we get around to realizing life is like that too. We have only so many hours in a day, only so much time and talent and ability, so much material possession to put to some use or other. Each man has to determine how much he can put in that size container. For every item we include we have to omit something else. We can't be chairman of every committee or active in every social or fraternal organization there is; we can't satisfy every whim for material possession and still contribute substantially to the work of the church and social agencies; we can't indulge in every kick that comes along and still be master of our faculties; we can't be models of self-denial and self-discipline by self-indulgence; we can't be pious playboys; devout and degenerate, saint and sinner. Some try and end up mostly miserable. That is always the consequence of trying to carry too much luggage.

We were preparing the evening meal when one of the ladies walked up to our campsite with an armload of canned food. "We brought more than we need," she said, "and we don't want to carry this all the way to Rock Harbor. Can you use it?"

With a dozen hungry teenagers, we could. She was thanked most sincerely, especially by the boys. Some of the items we added to the evening meal, and a small tin of honey we added to our store for the next day. The rest was left behind for some hiker who might be short of supplies or who would welcome a change. It would have been nice to take the extra food along, but we already knew where we were going and what we needed to get there.

an OAK of a MAN

He is like a tree planted by streams of water, that yields its fruit in its season, and its leaf does not wither.   Psalm 1:3

The righteous flourish like the palm tree, and grow like a cedar in Lebanon. They are planted in the house of the Lord, they flourish in the courts of our God.   Psalm 92:12, 13

I shall always remember a little hillside on the farm where I grew up. A grove of oak trees crowned its brow. They were not virgin timber, but they had stood there long enough to fight their way back to some semblance of what they could be if permitted to grow unmolested.

It wasn't a very large grove. I suppose there were not more than two dozen trees, but they seemed like more to me and my comrades from across the road. Here we played our games and picnicked through the happy days of boyhood. We chased the make-believe Indians around the trees, and in the shade of the largest oak we built our boy-sized model of the stone quarry we could see a half mile down the road. Here, in summer, the thick crop of acorns rolled like marbles beneath our feet, giving off a heavy, pungent odor as the hooves of cattle crushed those that fell into the hard path. It was a lovely spot and it has a high place in my memories.

But there are statelier oaks than those that the forest has to show us. I remember the man who used to walk through that grove of trees with me, my grandfather. We passed through it in the summer to pick blackberries in the pasture fields beyond, and in the fall as we hunted squirrels or rabbits; we walked those paths in the early spring to reach the fields beyond, where the ground was being prepared for sowing.

In every season of the year I passed beneath those mighty trees in the company of one who was an oak of a man. I saw in him all that a good tree would speak of—strong and straight and true, not only in his body but in his life and dealings with his fellowman; strong-rooted in his faith in God; fruitful in the acts of kindness that flowed out from him into the lives of others.

I can recall my first squirrel hunt, with him kneeling behind me, pointing over my shoulder so I would sight along his arm until I spotted the grey squirrel crouched against the limb of the tree. He showed me how to bait a fishhook and taught me to keep a sense of direction in the woods at night as we followed the sounds of the hunting dog. The vision of him kneeling by the straight-backed chair behind the stove has meaning because I knew that I was one of those for whom he prayed. I remember the high regard in which his neighbors held him, the faith they placed in his promises, the respect with which they listened to his judgments. He was an oak of a man.

The grove is gone now. A highway slashed through the trees. Those that it missed sleep beneath the blanket of the housing development that covers the hillside and the surrounding fields. The grove exists now only in my memories; there are dates set for the death of the greatest trees of the forest. Even the mighty redwood that has weathered the passage of twenty centuries will someday become again a part of the soil that gave it birth.

That other oak is gone now, too. A stone in a cemetery a couple of miles away tells me where we put his body. But he isn't there. There are no dates of death for those mighty growths called the children of God.

> He is like a tree planted by streams of water,
> That yields its fruit in its season,
> And its leaf does not wither.
>
> The righteous flourish like the palm tree,
> And grow high like a cedar in Lebanon.
> They are planted in the house of the Lord,
> They flourish in the courts of our God.
> Allelulia!

Father, we thank you for those lives that have touched our own and by their touching made us better than we would have been; for those who gave us memories that would ever make us become better than we are. Amen.

Thy word is true from the beginning: and every one of thy righteous judgments endureth for **ever.**

Psalm 119:160 (KJV)

the WINDS of GOD

One of the problems that man is facing in the urbanization of his world is the increasing distance he is placing between himself and nature. Man has an innate tendency to worship the creator of what he sees; and much of what modern man sees is man-made.

This is one of the reasons so much of the Bible is so unintelligible to us. The Bible is a book that sees God as very much present in his world. Biblical writers were surrounded by the creations of God. They walked paths of earth between canyons of stone and dirt, not in leisure, but of necessity; they looked at the heavens as much for direction as for speculation. Our paths are asphalt, our canyons concrete and steel, our guidance system electronic, and even our stars are neon.

Of course man is still dependent on the earth, but it is a very impersonal dependence. We are so far removed from the process that our dependence has become lost in the vast conglomeration of machines and computers. Modern man, with his sophisticated knowledge of science and evolution, thinks that once something has been explained it no longer holds any significance beyond itself; and he suffers from the great delusion that he has explained something when he has described it.

He laughs at the naïveté of his fathers, but he finds humor a poor substitute for faith. Like the poet who describes his childish ignorance in thinking the tops of the fir trees touched the sky, he must confess, "'tis little joy to know I'm farther off from heaven than when I was a boy." One can still find lessons in flowers or trees or the elements of nature; "books in the running brooks, sermons in stones," that sort of thing. It is the deeper fundamental lessons that we are prone to miss.

When a man spends any length of time in the out-of-doors, he soon discovers that there are certain things which he can change and must change if he is going to survive; but that there are other things which he cannot change and must work with. If a storm is brewing, for example, it does little good to wish the clouds would go away. One needs to decide whether he is going to travel with the storm, or against it, or take shelter from it. Progress can be made only by working within the larger framework of laws which are inevitable and unavoidable.

We can point with pride to man's achievements, many of which seem on the surface to be in defiance of the laws of nature; but always we find on closer analysis that we are not breaking laws, we are cooperating with them. Airplanes do not fly in opposition or violation with the law of gravity, but in cooperation with it.

That which is true in the realm of nature is true also in the realm of the spirit. There are laws of the spirit that are as immutable as the laws of nature. We ignore them, but we do so at our peril; just as we ignored the laws of conservation in our fields and reaped the dust bowls; just as we ignored the laws of sanitation and reaped polluted streams and air. Peace, brotherhood, love of one another are turning out to be far more than starry-eyed idealists' talk. They are the laws of survival for the human race. The great religions of the world have been saying, "Do it because it is right"; now society itself, with no pretense of religious motivation, is saying, "Do it because it is necessary."

If we are to survive, we must begin to cooperate with the inevitable. We can ignore the breezes of fashion and the currents of public opinion, but we must search the upper reaches for the winds of God. These we dare not ignore.

If a man begets a hundred children, and lives many years, so that the days of his years are many, but he does not enjoy life's good things, and also has no burial, I say that an untimely birth is better off than he.
Ecclesiastes 6:3 (KJV)

BURNING WATER

I used to think that the expression "she can't boil water without burning it" was a figure of speech to decry someone's cooking ability by ascribing to her the accomplishment of the impossible. I no longer believe that. I have burned water; in fact, I've done it several times on purpose and in large quantities.

The waters of the inland lakes on Isle Royale National Park are considered questionable for human consumption without boiling; and when you hike there with a dozen youths, you boil a lot of water. If you have never tasted water that has been boiled in an open pot over a wood fire for twenty minutes, you just haven't really lived! "Burned" is the only way I know to describe it.

The cause for the inconvenience is a small parasite that lives in the moose on the island and spends part of its life cycle in the waters of the lakes. The usual water purification tablets will not kill the parasite, so you are faced with the prospect of twenty minutes of boiling.

One of the rangers told me it would be relatively simple to get rid of the parasite; all they would have to do would be eliminate the twenty or so wolves that inhabit the island. The wolf is necessary for the completion of the cycle. The moose pick up the larvae from the water; in their body it becomes a form of tape worm which is relatively harmless to them. After a while the worm becomes incysted in the muscle or tissue of the moose; and when the wolves kill a moose and eat that tissue, the parasite enters still another stage in the body of the wolf, sometimes killing the wolf in the process. The eggs come from this last stage in the life cycle and pass out of the wolf's body into the water where the cycle begins again. By eliminating the egg-laying stage, the parasite could be eliminated; and hikers would no longer need to be advised to boil their water.

But there is another factor involved. The food supply of the moose on the island is limited. If the size of the herd becomes too large and they overpopulate the range, starvation and disease would wipe them out. As it is, the moose and the wolves have struck a balance. If man were to eliminate the wolf, he would find it necessary to take over the wolf's function and kill a certain number of moose every year, just as he now does in other areas where the balance of nature has been destroyed.

When man decides to play God in the elimination or change in a stage of life, his decision carries with it far more consequences than the immediate satisfaction of his whims. This fact has a great deal of meaning for some of man's most pressing social problems. The population explosion is one of the greatest, if not the greatest, world problem facing man today. We are working on many fronts to increase the number of people in the world. We are improving medical techniques to such an extent that thousands who would have died a few years ago can now be healed; we are increasing the care of mothers to such a degree that infant mortality is declining at a phenomenal rate; epidemics, which once swept entire cities or even continents, can now be controlled through sanitation and medication. The care of the aged and infirm has become such a science that the life expectancy has grown by several years.

We have become masters at the art of extending existence; but while we have succeeded in adding years to life, we have made little advancement in the art of adding life to years. We have made a god of existence itself. Our actions belie a belief in any meaningful existence beyond this one, and they often deny the importance of any meaning in this life outside survival. We are playing God every day in the sense of determining how long and under what conditions life shall exist. Such actions carry with them more responsibility than the satisfaction of the desire to live a long time. We must take some responsibility for all of life, not merely its continuation.

No one likes the taste of burned water, but the decision to have it otherwise is not one that can be made lightly.

And all these, though well attested by their faith, did not receive what was promised, since God had foreseen something better for us, that apart from us they should not be made perfect.

Hebrews 11:39, 40

FACES in the FIRE

There is something magic in a campfire. I have sat for hours and gazed into glowing embers, watching the shifting scenes and patterns of the red coals and the gray ashes. Sometimes it is the curious patterns themselves that fascinate me; at other times I see pictures of mountains or trees or animals; but most of all I see faces. Sometimes they are vague, unidentifiable faces— a nose, a mouth, two eyes, just faces. But at other times, if I watch long enough unhampered by conversation or interruption of any kind, I see other faces in the fire, faces that rise not so much from the burning of the fire before me as from the glowing of the embers of memory in the mind. The campfire only calls them as warmth calls to warmth.

The scientist has told us that fire is the radiance of the ages released from its imprisonment in time and space by the miner's pick, the driller's rig, or the woodsman's ax, and by the final touch of my match. Sunlight and nature were centuries accumulating the energy that the fire releases. We are really illuminating our darkness by the light of yesterday and warming ourselves with the energy of the past.

Perhaps this is why faces look back at us from the fire; the centuries have also accumulated the energy of the influence and examples of those who have gone before us, and now that too seeks to be released for our benefit. Our forefathers sensed a kinship with the flames. They too would enlighten our world.

In that grand adventure story by Jack London, *The Call of the Wild,* Buck the wolf dog was a creature of the wild. The urge of his wild heritage often pulled against his loyalty to John Thornton with a power that could hardly be resisted; but another power was greater—the love to his master. He had shared John Thornton's fire and looked into his face, and the love of his master bound him to the fire with chains he would not break:

Deep in the forest a call was sounding, and as often as he heard this call, mysteriously thrilling and luring, he felt compelled to turn his back upon the fire and the beaten earth around it, and plunge into the forest, and on and on, he knew not where or why; nor did he wonder where or why, the call sounding imperiously deep in the forest. But as often as he gained the soft unbroken earth and the green shade, the love of John Thornton brought him back to the fire again.

Is this not a parable of life? Are we not often tempted to give up the fight for human rights, for justice in government, for honesty in business, for integrity in our relationships, for all the specific ways in which goodness seeks to manifest itself in our world? Do we not often feel the call to a baser nature, to be unfaithful to the highest that we know? Are we not helped in our struggle by the knowledge that there are those who loved us and taught us better and gave us more than that which tempts us? Are we not called back to the fire? The ashes of the campfire shift and one by one the sparks go out; but ere the last coal ends its gleaming and the faces fade, there is a final thought that comes:

No man lives in this world forever. What shall we leave behind us when we are gone? What shall be the heritage that we pass on to those who sit by the equivalent campfires of the centuries to come hereafter? What faces shall look back at them from the fire?

the BEAUTY of DIFFERENCE

Having gifts that differ according to the grace given to us, let us use them.   **Romans 12:6**

Fall has long been my favorite season. I love the briskness that invades the air, the feel of the changing season, the smell of a campfire or burning leaves, the taste of apples picked from the tree, and, most of all, the glorious burst of color that dazzles the countryside.

When I began to list the things I enjoyed most about the fall of the year, I noticed that practically everything I listed was something that was not to be found in the other seasons. It was different, and its difference was what attracted me. The color of the trees is a good example. Springtime has its beauty as the misty green begins to quicken the greyness of the winter bareness of the branches; but it cannot compare with the beauty of fall when the red and yellow of the maples, the brown of the oaks, and the green of the spruce and cedar all comingle in a kaleidoscope of color that is breathtaking no matter how many times you see it. It would be much less interesting and far less beautiful if all the trees turned the same color before they shed their leaves. The beauty comes from the contribution each makes to the total scene.

The more I pondered the fact that it was difference that I found appealing, the more I realized that it is true of more than a season of the year. Vacations bring meaning and renewal of life because they offer us something different; therefore, what one man considers vacation, another man engages in for most of the year as *vocation*. Fashions and fads find their appeal through their differences from last year's styles and customs. Truly interesting conversation stems from groups in which different ideas are expressed, not in which everyone mirrors the opinions of the others in every detail. Was it Bob Hope who observed that the thing he liked most about the opposite sex was that it is so opposite?

All this has made me wonder whether we are making too much of a "thing" out of equality these days. We hear the word bandied about quite a bit. It runs the gamut from equal employment to equal education, to equality under the law, to equal power and equality of people. Most of the ideas seeking to be communicated have a great deal of validity in them, and the Gospels have quite a bit to say concerning some of the ideals that are fighting for current acceptance; but it is the word "equality" that I stumble on, mainly because I get the feeling that part of the time we are saying "equality" and implying "sameness."

Nothing could be farther from the truth. Whatever we mean when we speak of "all men being created equal," we surely cannot mean that all men are created the same. All we have to do is look at ourselves and look at the people we meet in one working day, and we know it isn't true. We are not equal in physical appearance. We are obviously not equal materially. We are not even the same emotionally. We are not equal in mental ability. In short, it might be said that the point at which we are the most equal is in our inequality. Each one is different. Each one of us is an individual in his own right; and the differences in physical, mental, material, and spiritual qualities are not particularly related. Physical and mental excellence go together as often as they are separated, in spite of our jokes about stupid athletes and dumb blondes. A man can be rich and religious or poor and unbelieving, or vice versa; and any combination of traits imaginable may be found in people regardless of race or nationality.

In the face of all this, we cannot seriously consider a doctrine of equality without what amounts to a limited definition of "equality." In fact, the message of the gospel is not so much a message of human equality as it is of human worth. It is a message of the love of God extended to the ten-talent man or the one-talent man; to the worker who has borne the burden in the heat of the day and the laborer hired at the eleventh hour; to a wealthy tax collector named Zacchaeus and a woman of the street named Mary Magdalene; to a highly educated Pharisee named Paul and an uneducated fisherman named Peter; and to a rich young ruler and a thief on a cross.

The good news is not that one man is the same as another; but that irrespective of talents and abilities and achievements all men are objects of God's love. Therefore I must not treat any man inconsiderately or cheaply, not because he is the same as myself but because *God has put worth on that man.*

This understanding must be the basis of any equality that we seek as Christians. Christian equality is not being expressed when everyone is doing the same work or receiving the same pay or eating the same food or walking lockstep in the same measured cadence of mediocrity. Christian equality is being achieved when every man under God is receiving the opportunity to be the best that he can be with whatever talents, whatever abilities, whatever limitations, and whatever differences he happens to possess. Until we achieve an honest recognition of this kind of equality, all our efforts to bring about other kinds of equality will continue to be bungling efforts.

Before the mountains were brought forth, or ever thou hadst formed the earth and the world, even from everlasting to everlasting, thou art God.

Psalm 90:2 (KJV)

the ETERNAL HILLS

One of the great thrills of my boyhood was the two weeks I spent camping in the Rocky Mountains. I had grown up in the foothills of the Appalachians and had always loved the mountains, and the majesty and beauty of the Rockies was an experience that I shall never forget. It came as something of a shock to learn that the Rockies were younger mountains than my familiar Appalachians. I had always supposed that it would take longer to make a pile of stone fifteen thousand feet high than it would to make one five thousand feet, and since the Rockies were so much higher, I had ignorantly assumed that they were also older.

It was then that I learned that mountains were not built from the outside by piling one rock on top of another; mountains are forced up from deep within the earth, the result of internal pressures and stresses. The outside forces of wind and rain and weather wear the mountains away; so as a mountain becomes older, it becomes smaller.

That thought disturbed me for a while. As a lover of the hills, I hated to think that there might come a day when there would be no more mountains to climb or gaze upon. Then I gained another bit of information; the process of wearing away is infinitely slow, but the process of mountain making is also a continual one. The pressures deep within the earth continue to force the earth's crust upward, creating new ridges and adding height to some of the old ones. Some of today's mountains may someday be smaller than they are, but they are not likely to disappear.

It would be more than a boy's imagination and dreams that would suffer if the hills were really to wear completely away. The rugged mountains are the sources of our fertile valleys. The breaking down of the rocks creates the soil that grows our food; the timbered slopes retain the moisture that feeds our streams to irrigate our fields; the rushing rivulets join themselves to others to become our mighty rivers. It is a story of life from death, for only as the mountains wear away can the valleys be built up; and it would be a very ungrateful piece of earth that despised the rocks that gave it birth because they are unable to bring forth corn and wheat. Our world needs those things that endure as well as those that change.

As it is in nature, so it is in society. There are ways and fashions that need to change, "lest one good custom should corrupt the world"; but there are also those things which must endure. No man has ever become better by becoming self-indulgent; no nation has ever become better by becoming more immoral; no society has ever endured once it has lost its sense of values.

It is not difficult to determine why certain values are held by certain groups if you do a bit of research into their culture. The significant point is that men of all cultures have felt that whatever their particular values are, they are worth preserving. What is it within man that causes him to feel that he ought to do right, even though he may disagree with other men as to what that right is? Why is it we find in man what Robert Louis Stevenson has called that

one thought, strange to the point of lunacy: the thought of duty; the thought of something owing to himself, to his neighbor, to his God: an ideal of decency, to which he would rise if it were possible; a limit of shame, below which, if it be possible, he will not stoop.

A sense of something owing; a sense of oughtness. When a man loses that, he has lost the essence of what it means to be a man. He has not only destroyed the hills that give him life, he has destroyed the sources from which the hills themselves arise.

The word of the Eternal came to Nathan: "Go and give my servant David this message from the Eternal. 'Are you to build me a temple to stay in? I have never stayed in a temple, not from the day that I brought the Israelites out of Egypt down to this day; I have always had my Dwelling in a tent.'"

II. Samuel 7:4-6 (Moffatt)

TENTS and TEMPLES

Mixed emotions is the only way to describe my feelings the day our Conference Camp Commission told me I could sell the old Baker tents we had used the past few years for trail camps and purchase new, lightweight tents with sewn-in bottoms and mosquito netting. I should have been happy since the permission was granted at my suggestion. The approval meant that we could now depend on sleeping undisturbed by the buzz and whine of hungry mosquitoes, black flies, and no-see-ums when we camped in territory they claimed as their own. In fact, I was happy about it; it was just that I hated to give up the flexibility that the Baker tents afforded. We could pitch them with a high ridge during the day and cook under the large canopy that extended out the front, or we could pitch them low and crowd six or even seven under shelter on a stormy night. That kind of flexibility was not going to be possible with our new tents. It was the old matter of trading flexibility for convenience and comfort. Thus my mixed emotions.

I have similar feelings when I consider what has happened to church buildings over the centuries. For three hundred years the sanctuary of the Jewish faith was a tent. It was quite a magnificent tent, to be sure, but still a tent, having for all its elaborateness some of the qualities shared by even the most humble piece of canvas—mobility, impermanence, and flexibility. It was during the time of the tent that the nation of Israel had its period of greatest unity. It was in this period that the Holy Land was won and the nation's boundaries extended. Their problems really started when they traded their tent for a temple.

The history of Christianity does not fare much better as far as temple trouble is concerned. Like the Jewish religion, the periods of the greatest vitality for the church have been its time of mobility—the meetings in the homes of the early Christians, like Priscilla and Acquila's of whom Paul writes; the gatherings in the market places; the borrowed or rented halls of Antioch and Athens; the secret conclaves in the catacombs of Rome.

Like the Jewish faith, Christianity has had its problems with buildings.

The cathedrals of Europe were built before the Reformation; John Wesley had to drag the church out into the fields and streets of England to get new life into it in his day, and today the crises and criticisms which the church faces follow on the heels of a great building boom. The structures themselves, like the Temple of Jerusalem, have been magnificent, and they will endure for hundreds of years; but somehow the vitality that was present in the times of the tent has difficulty surviving the atmosphere of the temple.

There is a passage of scripture in the Second Book of Samuel that tells of the desire of David to build a temple for the Lord after the conquest of the Holy Land. He has said to Nathan, "Here I stay in a house of cedar, while God's ark is inside the curtains of a tent!" He is evidently having guilt feelings about the difference between his own elaborate dwelling and the tabernacle which housed the Ark of the Covenant. So he resolved to build a temple, but the word of God came to him saying, "I have always had my Dwelling in a tent." What greater text could a camper ask for?

Perhaps there is something about tent dwelling that we need to remember when we move into temples, something that the nature of the surroundings makes more difficult to retain. Buildings give us such a false sense of achievement. They look so permanent, so everlastingly everlasting. Tents on the other hand, both by design and by construction, symbolize impermanence, mobility, and flexibility. They were made to be folded up and carried with you.

In the early years of the Jewish faith the tent brought God symbolically down off the mountain, saying to the people, "God is not THERE, he is HERE, . . . here with you, involved in your pilgrimage, moving through life with you." The Temple tended to return him to the THERE. Of course this was not the intention of temple building; but temples do have a way of implying that God is THERE and not in the midst of the life of his people.

Someone once wrote on a church that was to be torn down by urban renewal, "God don't live here any more!" There is a sense in which that statement can be written on the doors of any church, in any location, in any age. *God doesn't live there.* He is involved in the life of his people. To be sure, he is in the church when his people are, when they gather for worship and learning, for inspiration and guidance and for fellowship. But this is not his permanent address. He lives in a tent, and he pitches it where his people are.

I am not advocating a return to tents. We have the temples on our hands, and even the alchemy of modern science cannot change mortar into canvas. Besides, look at all the building codes that we would have to get rewritten, and the fire marshals we would have to fight! But if we can learn to live in temples with a tentlike spirit, if we can avoid feeling that we are bringing in the Kingdom when we paint another wall or add another room, if we can avoid becoming so tied to our old ways that we become as inflexible as the stones that wall us in; and if we can remember that here we have no permanent dwelling, that we seek a city that has foundations, whose builder and maker is God, then we may yet hope for the church and, through it, for our world.

Blessed is the man who trusts in the Lord. . . . He is like a tree planted by water, that sends out its roots by the stream, and does not fear when heat comes, for its leaves remain green, and is not anxious in the year of drought, for it does not cease to bear fruit. Jeremiah 17:7, 8

the CHARACTER of TREES

I shall never cease to marvel how an acorn knows to be an oak, especially a particular kind of oak. I shall never cease to marvel at the tiny spark of purpose that burns so resolutely deep inside a tree, telling it not only what to become, but telling it to become that insistently, relentlessly.

How wonderful if we would follow as well the purpose to which we are called to be sons of God! It would be something even grander if man would do it, for a tree does not have to decide to become a tree. That is built in. But man is given freedom to choose between good and evil, between God and self, and it is a far greater thing to become something out of choice than because there is nothing else to become.

And yet, it would be a mistake to think that because the process is automatic, it is easy. Have you ever considered what chance any particular acorn has in becoming a tree? It must first find a place in the earth that is soft enough for it to penetrate and in the process escape the squirrel, the deer, and the cattle that seek it out for food. It must accomplish this in a suitable growing season and then compete with others for sunlight and moisture. As it breaks through the ground, it faces again the search of animals for tender plants to eat. If it reaches thumb-size and upward, there are the boys who look for walking sticks or fishing poles; and of course there are always the ravages of wind and fire and the crushing weight of other trees that fall.

Perhaps the tree's secret lies in its ability always to point toward the sunlight. No matter how steep the hillside on which you find them, trees always seem to point toward the sun. Walking through the woods, I have found them bent nearly to the ground from some accident in their youth, yet turning ninety degrees upon themselves and pointing upward still.

When we consider the difficulty of their becoming, we see it as a role we would scarcely envy; and yet, it is precisely this struggle that gives them strength. A tree that finds it easy misses something. I have seen trees that attained their growth too easily. I have walked through the woods and found great giants stretched upon the ground, broken branches littering the forest floor and hanging from the limbs of their stronger neighbors.

I used to wonder why they fell, while apparently weaker trees still stood. Finally I noticed their roots. These were seeds that fell on extremely fertile, marshy ground. The soil was easy to penetrate, the moisture was readily available, and so the trees had spread their roots thinly over the surface. They had grown rapidly as long as all was quiet, but soon they had more above the ground than they had rootage to support, and the slightest wind was able to topple them.

There is much to be said for growing through struggle, at least enough struggle to require that we penetrate the surface of life to something deeper.

SOUNDS in the SILENCE

The Lord was not in the wind; . . . the Lord was not in the earthquake; . . . the Lord was not in the fire; . . . and after the fire a still small voice.   I Kings 19:11, 12

A few summers ago I sat with a group of youth on a high point of land overlooking a bend in the beautiful Potomac. Far below us across the river, a broad valley stretched away to the foothills which faded into the horizon. The sun was setting and a nighthawk sailed across the graying sky. From the woods behind us a thrush poured out his evening song. The leader of the group was a wise man. He made no speeches about the beauty of the spot but let it speak for itself in the language it knew best—the voice of stillness. He suggested that we sit there for a while and listen. You know, I could really *feel* the machinery of life slowing down and growing quiet. Soon I felt more than the pure beauty of the surroundings. I think I knew a bit of what the psalmist meant when he said, "Be still, and know that I am God."

I have often thought since that day how much we miss because we do not have or take the time to sit down and be still. Let me ask you a question: How long has it been since you sat down for the sake of being silent for even a few minutes? Don't count time reading a book or watching television or listening to music. When was the last time you sat down for the express purpose of being still and listening? It is a frustrating question, isn't it? You immediately feel like asking, But what do you do? and that is precisely the point. You sit down, and you be still! And how little of it we do!

I saw a perfect example of the haste and hurry of our day on one of our Christmas shopping trips to a large department store. We were elbowing our way down the aisle when I happened to glance over at the escalator, and there he was—a man running up the escalator. We just can't get there fast enough! You lose one turn in a revolving door and your schedule is shot for the entire day. It's rush, rush, rush from the first gulp of coffee in the morning to the last exhausted sigh at night.

Even our prayers are relegated to the drag end of the day when we gasp out a few hurried petitions or thank-yous and tumble into bed without even waiting to see if there is any reply. Our world is far too busy and far too noisy. We need to have a time of quietness in which to still our souls and receive the strength that comes to us in quietness and confidence.

Of course, all silence is relative. The only absolute silence you could have would be in a vacuum, but there is a kind of silence you can achieve. Walk into a little patch of woods some place and sit down for a few minutes. When you first stop everything may seem absolutely quiet, but if you wait a few minutes you will begin to hear sounds that you never realized were there before. A birdsong will float to you over the stillness; an insect may begin chirping at your feet. Did you know that you can hear a leaf fall? Everyone has heard the wind howling around the house or roaring in the branches of the trees, but do you know its song among the grasses of the field? It does not require much sensitivity to hear the rain on a tin roof, but are you acquainted with its gently falling upon the bare earth?

As there are sounds about us that can be heard only after we pass through the veil of silence, so there are sounds which are peculiar to the spirit; and only when we have entered into the silence of communion with God can we hear their message. Surely this is the reason Jesus had his times of drawing apart from the press of the multitudes. It was in these moments that he found the messages others were too busy and too noisy to hear.

When I think of the lessons to be learned in silence, I think of the prophet Elijah and the events recorded in the nineteenth chapter of the First Book of Kings. The story pictures him in the mountains, where he has fled in terror to escape the wrath of Jezebel. The experiences through which he had passed were quite different from those we might go through today; but the feeling of exhaustion and frustration he expressed sounds rather familiar: I have had enough; . . . O Lord, take now my life away, for I am mortal, as my fathers were. All others have forsaken thee, and I am left alone to do the work that needs to be done. I have had all that I can stand. Let there be an end to my struggles!

Does it sound vaguely familiar? Forget the circumstances and examine only the feelings expressed, and it sounds as though it might have been overheard on Main Street, U.S.A. Many of us, whether we have used the words of Elijah or not, have felt the pressure and press of the busy world in which we live. It was to this tired and weary man that God spoke, not in earthquake or fire or wind, but in "a voice of gentle stillness."

Silence is not an end in itself. It is not suggested that we find a quiet hillside and spend the rest of our days in meditation. Through silence we receive the strength to serve. Elijah learned that there were two kings for him to anoint and a prophet to mark as his successor. This is not in contradiction of what has just been said and have us all go charging out again, forgetting to receive our directions. Our world needs service, and its need is for the kind of service that has been prepared for in the silence in which God speaks. Then when we go out to labor, we shall know that we do his bidding; and we will not be alone. That which came to Elijah can come to us as well; for that which God has spoken once echoes continually in the hills of silence, "Be still . . . and know that I am God."

Carry one another's burdens and so live out the law of Christ.

Every man must "shoulder his own pack."

Galatians 6:2, 5 (Phillips)

HAIR CURLERS and HAND CREAM

The girls were all in a dither. We had finished our shakedown hike in preparation for the real thing a few weeks away, and they were engaged in the painful process of deciding what had to stay behind and what they would take with them. The pile of discards was impressive and the current discussion centered around a collection of cosmetics—hair curlers, shampoo, and hand cream. Anyone could have told them they were luxury items, not necessities. They knew that themselves. That wasn't the problem. The problem was, they still wanted to take them.

So here were the girls, having learned that a pack which feels bearable and looks acceptable at the beginning of the day can become downright burdensome by the time you hike a few miles over rough terrain; trying to figure out how to live with their new knowledge without giving up all their luxuries. You might have guessed they would come up with something that would enable them to have their cake and eat it too. They did it this way: one girl brought the shampoo, one brought the hand lotion, and each one brought a few curlers. That way they could lighten their load and still enjoy what on a trail hike they felt would be a real luxury. They still had to decide who would use the curlers and when, but they could only do it by sharing. The concept of "mine" and "yours" at some point had to give way to "ours." It wasn't a matter of everyone owning everything; it was a lesson in the individual and the community living in mutual responsibility.

I thought of two verses of scripture, both from the sixth chapter of Paul's letter to the Christians at Galatia, "Carry one another's burdens and so live out the law of Christ," and, "Every man must 'shoulder his own pack.'" Much of our current difficulty in society stems from our persistence in attempting to separate those ideas. We have said "bear one another's burdens" and developed all sorts of sociological and psychological excuses to gloss over the responsibility of the individual for the choices he makes in life. We have used "every man must shoulder his own pack" to argue against social work and welfare programs. Much of our world seems in danger of forgetting the

71

need to bear our brothers' burdens, and the rest of it seems bent on ignoring individual responsibility. The two ideas make very good checks and balances, but neither one is adequate as the basis of a system.

The first statement, "bear one another's burdens," hardly needs any commentary as a basic principle of the Christian faith. Add to it such passages as "we that are strong ought to bear the burden of the weak," and "inasmuch as you have done it to the least of these," and you have the tenets of the faith which have resulted in the establishment of hospitals, schools, orphanages, homes for the aged, and all manner of welfare organizations. One would be hard pressed to find any such organization that was not influenced, directly or indirectly, by the Christian faith. But there is more here than a statement of the bias of a particular religion.

Man shall either learn to live with his brother and bear his burdens; or, like the gingham dog and the calico cat, they will eat each other up. Bearing one another's burdens also calls to my attenion the fact that I, too, am a dependent creature. There is no room here for a superior, self-righteous attitude. There are others who carry some of my burdens.

There is also the matter of everyone shouldering his own pack. The packs may not be of equal weight or contain the same thing, but there is such a thing as taking too much responsibility for another human being. A man needs a sense of responsibility for himself along with my sense of responsibility for him. One of our problems in our approach to poverty has been our unwillingness to let the poor be responsible; it is less bother to keep them dependent—perhaps more expensive, but less bother. Jesus said, "It is more blessed to give than receive." Are we not denying the poor the greater blessing when we constantly force upon them the role of receiver?

The trail brings into vivid focus the relationship between the individual and the group. When I sit down in the evening after a long, hot hike, I look around at the equipment leaning against the trees and I notice that it isn't all the same. Some is borrowed and some is owned; some are the newest frame knapsacks, others are the older but still serviceable models; some sleeping bags are lightweight and compact, others are bulky and heavier; but the fellow with the lighter pack can carry more of the food or equipment, so his advantage becomes the group's advantage. Each evening you eat food that has been carried by different members of the group and cooked over a fire that has been a group effort; at night, rolled in a sleeping bag you have carried yourself, you sleep in a tent that was carried by one member and is held down by stakes and ropes from another pack. You are both giver and receiver; responsible for others and one for whom others are responsible. Is not such living the essence of Christian community?

to BUILD a FIRE

Don't throw away your trust now—it carries with it a rich reward in the world to come. Patient endurance is what you need if, after doing God's will, you are to receive what he has promised.   Hebrews 10:35, 36 (Phillips)

Sometimes one learns more from failure than success. Have you ever looked at a pile of ashes and tried to figure out what made it a good fire? If you want to know that, you have to study the ones that failed and profit from their failure.

I remember one morning when I served on a scout initiation team. It was our job to go around and gather up the young men whom we had deposited in the woods the night before. Each scout had brought with him his bedroll, a knife, and two matches. His task was to spend the night alone in the woods with no light and no other scout around him. Before he made his bed and crawled in for the night, he was to build a fire. In most instances

75

we found a pile of ashes on the ground that gave testimony to the fact that a good fire had been built and kept going for a while. Some of the other ashes told another story, a story of an effort that had failed.

I noticed there were three kinds of failure. Some failed for lack of tinder. We looked at a couple of sites where there were practically no ashes. The fires had never really gotten started because there had been no preparation. There were no shavings, no tiny twigs to catch the first flame of the match. The scout had grabbed a handful of twigs and held a match against them, and so we found nothing but the charred twigs and the burned-out matches. The fire had gone out almost before it started because there was no tinder.

I would suggest that this is quite often a reason for failure in life, the lack of the proper materials to catch the spark and nourish it and to keep it going until there is enough heat generated to ignite the larger twigs and branches. This seems to be the hardest lesson to learn in fire building. There is a tendency to skip the groundwork and start in the middle.

Life offers the same temptation. Our society does not tend to produce much patience. We are a "I-want-what-I-want-when-I-want-it" people. I remember counseling with a young man who wanted to quit school and get a job in a service station. Now there is nothing wrong with working in a service station, mind you; but he was not seeking this work because he had skill as a mechanic and saw this as a way of fulfilling it, or because he had a family to feed and this was an available means of support. He simply wanted a shortcut. He wanted to leave out the tinder and throw on the logs—to get wheels, to have money, to be a big shot. He wanted to light a log with a match. He had to learn that life doesn't catch on that way.

As we made our rounds that morning, I found that lack of tinder was not the only reason that fires did not burn. We found instances where there had been a good pile of shavings. The little pile of soft grey ashes and stub ends of twigs gave evidence of that. The young man had spent his time of preparation well; he had whittled his shavings until there were plenty of them to catch the spark and keep it going; but he had left out the kindling. He had tried to go from shavings to logs, and you don't light logs from shavings any more than you light kindling from matches. You need the tinder to catch the spark and then the kindling to generate the heat to ignite the logs.

What kindling is to a fire, persistence is to a life. The bigger the log you want to burn, the more persistence you need to get it started. Again, what is true in building a fire is true in building a life. Our instant philosophy of living does not make for persistence much more than it makes for preparation.

Abraham Lincoln was a man who knew a great deal about fire building. In his day it was a part of daily living. His life reflects the lessons he learned in the process. The presidency of these United States is a rather sizable log to burn, and he didn't light it from a handful of shavings. There were long years of preparation and study; then there was the persistence with which he pursued his goal until he achieved it, facing failure after failure in the process. We remember him for the logs he burned, but there was a lot of kindling gone to ashes before the log ignited.

We saw a third kind of fire that morning. These were fires that had had a good start. The tinder had been there and the kindling too; but again, you could tell by the ashes that the fire had not burned very long. The reason was quite evident. The scouts had failed to collect any larger fuel. They never bothered to look around to find something big enough to provide enough substance to the fire so that it could really serve a purpose. The fire had had a good beginning; it had gone out because there was nothing left to burn.

How many lives have you seen like that? Lives that start off with a great beginning, good preparations, promise of something worthwhile, only to peter out with nothing left to burn, no purpose to keep them going. We talk a lot these days about the temptations of youth, and youth has its problems;

but we need to recognize as well the temptations of middle age, of lives that go out halfway through their usefulness because the person did not have a goal that was substantial enough to last very long. Whatever the occupation may be, if it is just a way to make a living, it soon loses its interest and its power. Whether it is found in the job itself or in an avocation aside from our source of support, life needs more fuel than existence if it is to burn very long. This is the most tragic failure of all, a fire gone out because there was nothing left to burn.

You can build many kinds of fire in life. Each fire has its own usefulness, but no matter which kind we build, the principles are the same. We need the tinder of preparation, the kindling of persistence, and the fuel of purpose. Someday history will look at the ashes we have left and judge our effort at building a fire. If we have succeeded, there will be the ashes of a life well lived to mark our victory. If we have failed, those who come after us will read our lack in the charred remains.

Jesus said to him, "No one who puts his hand to the plow and looks back is fit for the kingdom of God."

Luke 9:62

the MIDDLE MILE

You can say what you please about the difficulty of getting started on a project and the hard task of finishing it once it has been begun; but on the trail the hardest part of the hike isn't the beginning or the ending—it's the middle.

Everyone starts off with enthusiasm and new energy from the fellowship around the campfire and the night's rest; and when the destination is in sight, you can always summon up the reserves of strength for that last spurt into the new camp. It's the long miles in between the start and the conclusion that call for real determination. You can feel it in a group. The first two or three miles of a day's hike are often marked by friendly conversation back and forth; sometimes there is even breath enough for singing as we hike. The last mile or so quite often shares the same enthusiasm, as the prospect of a swim in the lake or loafing in the sun before preparations for the evening meal lifts everyone's spirit. But in between there comes a time of heavy silence, when little talking takes place and attempts at singing result in solos that end prematurely.

It does not take either a prophet or the son of a prophet to observe that what is true of a group of hikers on the trail is also true of personal living and of the course of great causes. Youth has its enthusiasms and ideals to get it started; old age has its patience and its longer view of history to sustain it; but the years in between often bring their peculiar problems, when one has nearly faded and the other has not yet come into being.

It doesn't require a great deal to get a home started; but keeping it going takes a bit of doing. It is a long way from the joy of bringing a child into the world and the joy of bouncing grandchildren on your knee. The poet William Pratt has said concerning the golden wedding anniversary, "Crops are rich when two have planted love." And so they are; but to jump from the planting to the harvest is to ignore the season of cultivation, and that is where much of the work comes in.

What is true of personal living is equally true of great causes. Between a great beginning and a glorious ending lies the difficult task of enduring. A hundred years ago we made a great start in freeing a people. The movement was launched with trumpets blaring and flags flying. We look forward to a day when the black man and the white man can live and work and worship together in harmony and brotherhood. We are walking now that most unromantic but necessary middle mile without which the beginning is meaningless and the end impossible.

The steps we take on the trail to help us endure the middle mile might offer us some help in life's harder hikes. First, we take a rest. Not too long a rest, or the muscles will stiffen up and the going will be more difficult than ever, but enough of a rest that we can catch our breath.

The second thing we do is find a refreshing view or new experience which will enrich the resting. It may be a high point from which we can look over the miles already traveled or gaze into the distance where the horizon swallows up the landscape in haze; it may be a patch of blueberries or wild strawberries to pick or a stand of wild flowers to enjoy; it may be the singing of a song or the laughter of good fellowship. Whatever particular form it takes, if it brings refreshment to the spirit, it also brings new vigor to the body.

The third thing we do is think of the goal. The evening by the lake, the tents pitched for the night, a bedroll spread in a sunny spot for a nap before the evening meal, the smell of food and the crackle of the campfire—getting one's mind off the difficulties of the moment and getting another glimpse of the distant goal bring new life to tired bodies.

Finally, we learn to concentrate on one step at a time. That is the hardest part. It is tempting to stay with the resting and thinking about the ultimate goal; but there is also the time for the grim and tiring business of putting one foot in front of another, . . . concentrating on making it to the next hill top, the next bend in the trail. Such progress may be slow, but it is steady.

Some hikers never learn that lesson. They think the entire journey can be conducted with the same burst of speed with which they started. You usually find them strewn out along the trail; not resting and ready to go on but exhausted, wrung out from attempting to make a cross-country journey into a hundred-yard dash.

The mortality rate in the middle mile is rather high. Only those who have learned the secret of true patience, which is the delicate balance between inactivity and frantic action, find the fulfillment of the promise: "They that wait upon the Lord shall renew their strength; they shall mount up with wings as eagles; they shall run, and not be weary; and they shall walk, and not faint."

I lift up my eyes to the hills.   Psalm 121:1

I have never done any real mountaineering; but during the past few summers I have enjoyed hiking to the highest point in each state in which we have camped, Mt. Washington in New Hampshire, Mt. Marcy in New York, and Spruce Knob in West Virginia. This has been enough to make me aware that there is some peculiar affinity between the soul of man and the hills of earth.

One of the best known British climbers has described this fascination as "some quality in a hill which defies analysis. Call it the spirit of the hill, call it anything you like, but no one has yet explained why it is hills have a power over men." This same mystery was reflected by Sir George Mallory who, when asked why men climb mountains, replied, "Because they are there."

The challenge of the mountains is certainly part of the answer of their attraction. It is impossible to look at them long without feeling their pull, even if we never climb them. There is a challenge in their very being there. Mount Everest has so challenged men for decades. It was really about this mountain that Mallory made his famous statement, and it was the challenge of this mountain that eventually took his life.

I used to think it was such an awful waste of life to die climbing mountains, but now I am not so sure. I see it in another light. The urge to conquer mountains is that in man which responds to challenge. The climbers of mountains are related to those who have endured hardships to find new lands and spread man's knowledge to the stars; they are akin to those who labor in the fields of science and medicine to conquer disease; they know the loneliness of those who seek to right the social evils of the world. Their heartbeat echoes in the breasts of men and women who struggle in silence to climb the slopes of disappointment and loneliness and despair. Our world would be a poor place indeed were it not for such men and women whose spirit rises up to respond to the challenge of our world.

It is not only the challenge of the hills that calls; the intenseness of the fellowship such striving demands adds its attraction. Mountain-climbing is no task for solitary individuals. I have read that there is a sign on one of the foot trails leading to Pike's Peak that reads, "No solitary hikers beyond this point. Only experienced climbers, bound together, should attempt the climb."

The world reads in the headlines of its newspapers the names of one or two men who may set foot on the summit of a mountain like Everest, but the victory is possible only through the efforts of a team. There were three hundred porters in the team that conquered Everest. Hugh Rutledge, in *The Conquest of Everest*, has written, "Above all else I should like to stress our unity as a party. This was undoubtedly the biggest single factor in the final

89

result, for the ascent of Everest demanded a very high degree of selfless co-operation; . . . the story of Everest is one of teamwork."

Mountain men have known for centuries what the rest of the world is very slow in finding out. There is no room in any of life's great achievements for selfish individuals. Only when we are willing to put aside the provincialism involved in so many of our international disputes, the pride of racism, the pettiness of our political party loyalty, the narrowness of our denominationalism, can we expect to scale the heights of human need that confront our world. We have reached the point beyond which no solitary hikers can proceed.

There is also the inspiration with which the mountains reward those who climb. Not a little of their inspiration stems from the fact that they remind us of all that we have not yet attained; majestic fingers pointing us away from ourselves, directing us to the heights. But, oh, the view that awaits those who conquer!

There is something grand and glorious in a view from the heights. Even the satisfaction of achieving is lost in the vision stretched out before you. There is no pride for man in such a spectacle. Men climb and the view is there, something given. Man does not create it. He can scarcely even take it in.

There is a great deal of satisfaction involved in cresting the summit of a mountain, but the feeling which remains the longest is that of feeling your smallest after you have expended your greatest effort and achieved. One of the youths who hiked with me one day put it this way, "It makes you feel real small, but a part of something." Who wouldn't climb a mountain to feel like that?

ACORNS and OAK LEAVES

God has chosen what the world calls foolish to shame the wise; he has chosen what the world calls weak to shame the strong. He has chosen things of little strength and small repute, yes and even things which have no real existence to explode the pretensions of the things that are.   I Corinthians 1:27, 28 (Phillips)

Have you noticed how the most colorful season of the year dumps us rather unceremoniously into the dullest and drabbest days of the calendar?

Fall is beautiful beyond description with all the glorious color of the trees and the lovely autumn days that accompany them; and winter, once it arrives in all its fury, can be beautiful too. But the days in between are some of the dullest and drabbest of all. The skies are a dull, listless gray; the wind whines around the house and seeks out the loose windowpanes. Often a cold rain adds to the discomfort. There are not even any leaves left on the trees to give us hope. Everywhere we look there is only bareness and desolation. It is a season that apparently has little to recommend it and little in it to offer much of promise of better things to come. The days are growing shorter; the hours of darkness are winning in their battle over the daylight. No wonder the latter part of December has been celebrated for centuries with festivals and rejoicing; this is the time when the shortest day has finally arrived, and the tide begins slowly to creep the other way. Light is proving to be victorious over darkness.

No wonder the early Christians chose this season to honor the coming of Christ into the world. How appropriate to choose the darkest hour to hail the coming of light. What could be a more fitting time to celebrate the birth of him who was hailed as the light of the world? Men had rested their hopes on the glory that was Rome and the imperial might of her armies, but the brightness of that glory had dimmed. The power that was Rome was a sickness unto death, even as the glory that is autumn is a sign of life running out. While men were gazing in wonder at the transient beauty that attracted their attention because of its show and color, God was preparing something less spectacular but far more lasting.

Man, as usual, was so fascinated with the leaves on the trees that he never noticed the acorns beneath his feet. But, as is so often the case, that which is regarded as insignificant was to prove to be the most essential. Men sing their songs to the beauty of the leaves, but it is from the acorns that the forests of the future come. In fact, for all their beauty the leaves will serve the interests of acorns, providing cover and mold on the forest floor to give shelter and sustenance to the germ of life that waits its moment of sunlight and soil to burst forth upon the world.

God has often shunned that which is showy and transient or used it to prepare the way for the coming of something much more lasting; and often that from which the lasting comes is rather insignificant in its appearance, has no particular beauty in its form and, like the acorn, may even be acrid and bitter to the taste. "God has chosen what the world calls foolish to shame the wise; he has chosen what the world calls weak to shame the strong. He has chosen things of little strength and small repute, yes and even things which have no real existence to explode the pretensions of the things that are." So wrote the apostle Paul twenty centuries ago, and he was a man who ought to know.

Men looked for deliverance in empires such as Rome and despised a child not of royal blood; men sought a Messiah after the kingship of David and refused a Messiah who came to serve and suffer and eventually die.

> They were all looking for a king
> To slay their foes and lift them high;
> Thou cam'st, a little baby thing
> That made a woman cry.

Nor has the analogy of Christmas ceased to be. New life still comes from bitter fruit. A life is struck by tragedy, and from the anguish of the spirit arises a new sensitivity to people and their needs; a church passes through days of desperation and discouragement and in the midst of its struggle to exist finds a purpose for existence and a reason for being; a city passes through the fire and blood of a rebellion and in its wake rises a new spirit of brotherhood; a nation searches its conscience about its involvement in Viet Nam and out of the differences of opinion comes a new sense of the meaning of democracy; a world wrestles with the problems of learning to meet together at conference tables instead of over gun barrels and launching pads and comes at last to an understanding of peace.

Not all these things have come to pass; but they are the acorns of new life that are scattered over the wilderness of life, buried beneath the glitter of missiles, the feet of armies, the concrete of our cities, and the weight of our preoccupations. How long the seed will lie there before it germinates and produces life, I do not know; but I know it's there.

Lo, these are but the outskirts of his ways; and how small a whisper do we hear of him!
Job 26:14

The campfire was nearly gone and we were losing our struggle with the encroaching darkness. It was our first night in the interior of the island that is a national park off Michigan's northern shore. Our tents were pitched a few yards from Chickenbone Lake that reflected the fading light in its mirrored surface, giving us the illusion that we might be holding off the night. A backward glance at the woods or across the lake at the outline of the trees against the sky told us that it wasn't so.

From out on the lake there came a weird and plaintive cry like a lost soul seeking solace from our light. I was fully expecting the whispered, "What was that?" which came from two or three throats at once. There is nothing quite like the cry of a loon at night on a lonely northern woods' lake to break your mind loose from the moorings of our sophisticated way of thinking and send it hurtling through the past when man was moved to feelings of awe and wonder by such sounds. Here there were no magic switches to throw and hold back the primal questions that live far nearer the surface of the mind than we care to think.

Today mystery is suspect. Our world view, on the surface at least, is one of questioning, of suspicion and skepticism. I suppose in the long run it is a good thing. For too long the world walked in the darkness of fear and super-stition. Man was afraid of the unknown; he lived in the shadows of half-truths and deliberate falsehood, the pawn of anyone who could perform what seemed to be the impossible. How the tide of useful knowledge was held back by the barriers of fear and superstition! What activities have been perpetuated because of man's worship of the mysterious! The worship of the unknown has been a good thing to outgrow.

And yet, there are times when I wonder if we have gone too far. Not that I would have us return to the dark ages; but to give up our fear of the unknown is one thing, to sacrifice our sense of awe and wonder as well is something else. I have a feeling that part of the dilemma of our world today stems from this. Our curiosity has gained for us new knowledge; but our loss of awe and wonder has taken with it our sense of humility, and knowledge without humility is a dangerous thing.

Like Moses and the burning bush, we need the time of turning aside to observe; but there is also a time for standing in wonder and humility. Without the turning aside there can be no new knowledge, but without the bowing in wonder there can be no proper use of the knowledge that is revealed.

I have noticed that those who really see something of the nature of our world see deep enough to have more awe and wonder instead of less. It is only the self-styled expert who skims the surface of knowledge that loses his sense of reverence. A Russian astronaut circled the earth in his spacecraft and announced to the world that he had looked and there was no God. Albert

Einstein, the man who perhaps more than any other in our age comprehended something of the vastness of the earth, sat in a sailboat with a friend of mine in a lake in the mountains of western Maryland and said, "John, how can anyone not believe in God?"

Scientists are now telling us that they will soon create life in a test tube. Perhaps they will. I, for one, shall not be particularly disturbed by that fact. What I shall be more interested in knowing is what the scientists will do when they discover it.

I have no fear of any knowledge man can gain if it is gained in humility. It is when man seeks knowledge without humility that I shall be afraid—afraid for man and the future of his world. For knowledge without humility is the beginning of destruction.

But when he came to himself. . . .   Luke 15:17

Being lost can be a very frightening thing. I remember the winter in the mountains of central West Virginia when a group of us drove a few miles back into the hills and camped for a few days to try our luck at deer hunting. It was the afternoon of the third day of the season, and my friend and I had split up in order to cover a little more territory. Rather late in the day a brisk snowstorm blew in and for several minutes filled the air with great flakes like shredded cotton candy, which blotted out visibility for more than a few yards in any direction. The wind that carried them blew them into my face and eyes until it was useless to try either to walk or watch, so I found a large tree and crowded myself against it on the sheltered side and waited out the storm.

While I was standing there huddled against the trunk, two deer bounded over the rise of the hill a few yards in front of me. They saw me as quickly as I saw them and stood like statues for a few seconds before disappearing into the snow. One whirled and was quickly gone back the way it had come. The other ran on in the direction they had been traveling when they spotted me.

I figured that the one that went back the way it had come was headed toward the laurel thickets where they had spent the day; but if my memory served me right, there were old fields in the direction the other one was traveling, and I thought I might have a chance of putting venison in the freezer before the day was up.

When the little storm had blown itself out, I took up the trail. I had not gone very far before I realized that the deer had changed direction and was veering away from the fields I had thought of, but I decided to stick to the trail for awhile anyway. Somewhere down the mountain I felt sure its trail would cross the old log road that would lead me back to our tent. Finally I saw an opening in the brush some distance below me and what I took to be the road I was looking for. I left the tracks, never having had another glimpse of the deer after it disappeared from sight into the blowing snow.

I knew something was wrong when I stepped out on to the old road. It was really little more than two overgrown paths a few feet apart where the forest had not yet reclaimed the scar left by timbering operations many years before. The road we had camped beside, while certainly no throughway, was traveled in the fall and winter by a few hunters in jeeps to reach the more inaccessible sections of the woods, but this one showed no signs of use by any vehicle at all, only a few tracks of hunters.

I had hunted in the same section for several falls and one winter before, but I had no idea where this road came from or where it went. From what I knew of mountain trails such as this, I knew that one direction would probably lead me eventually to a better road and that road eventually to a house or farm; the other end would wander on for miles and likely stop at the remains of an old sawmill. But which direction led to which? I had less than an hour before dusk would settle in, and darkness follows quickly in the mountains.

These thoughts flashed through my mind as I realized that I was lost. I had no desire to stumble along through the mountains without a light. I thought for a moment of going back up the hill I had just descended to one of the large rock outcroppings I had passed and gathering in enough wood to keep a good fire going for the night. I was dressed warmly and it would not have been too uncomfortable. But I knew there would be some worried friends back at camp if I chose that course of action, so I voted it down for the moment.

I looked again at the footprints in the snow. The few flakes of new snow had made it hard to tell for sure how old the tracks were, but there was one set that looked as though they might have been made early that morning. If so, the hunter who had made them might just be returning the way he had gone. I made a lucky guess. I had not gone very far until I met him coming out. I told him where we were camped and he knew the territory well enough to give me directions. I was only about a mile from camp, most of it nearly straight up.

Well, to use a lot less breath in telling than I did in climbing, I made it back up the mountain and on to the old log road that led to camp a little before dark, and into camp before my friends had worried much.

The experience taught me a few lessons about wandering around in the wilderness—like the importance of taking more note of where I was going and consulting a compass for directions now and then. But the most important lesson I learned about getting lost was that being lost is not a matter of distance. It is a matter of relationship; it is a matter of where you are in relation to where you ought to be. You can be lost very close to home. Furthermore, being found doesn't necessarily imply that you have arrived at your destination; it simply means you have some idea where you belong.

For the Son of man came to seek and to save the lost.   Luke 19:10

DRIFTWOOD

I remember a summer in New Hampshire when we spent most of one afternoon picking up pieces of driftwood left high and dry by the spring floods. We enjoyed looking at them and imagining forms and figures in the gnarled and twisted shapes. With some of them it was not a matter of making them into something else at all, but just enjoying the intricate patterns and grain of the wood, washed and rubbed by sand and water and bleached by wind and sun.

I have asked myself what it is about driftwood that makes it so fascinating. How can one see something beautiful in something old and worn and weathered? I have found two things. One is the scars that are found in the pieces of wood. The fiber, the gnarls, and the weathering of elements form a pattern that is unique and distinctive. Experience leaves its marks in lives as well as in wood. Lives that have sorrow can often be the most comforting; hearts that have known loneliness can be the greatest companions; those that have conquered hardship offer the greatest inspiration.

There is another factor, too: there is the eye of the beholder. I confess that my wife had a keener eye for much of this than I did. Some of the things she saw in the pieces I did not see until she called them to my attention. There were even a few that she could see that I never did make out. It is always so. A great part of the beauty of anything is found in the eye of the beholder. Our Lord looked on lives and saw things others couldn't see. They said of him, "He eats with sinners." Their ridicule became his glory. He saw in people not merely what they were but what, by the grace of God, they could be.

It occurred to me, that our Lord was a collector of driftwood. What an eye he had for ferreting it out, half buried in the sand or hidden in the tangles of life. What specimens he found! There was one named Mary Magdalene, washed to his very feet by the wave of hatred and accusation, claimed to have been taken in the very act of adultery. Her accusers waited for him to pass judgment upon her. He stooped and wrote in the dust forgotten words. Some have suggested that they were such words as "pride," "arrogance," "greed," "prejudice." At any rate, as he wrote them he said, "Let him who is without sin among you be the first to throw a stone at her"; and when he looked up all the accusers had drifted away.

What an object of beauty and inspiration that bit of driftwood became— her adoration in the house of Simon the Pharisee as she bathed his feet with her tears and dried them with her hair; her vigil at the cross with his mother and that little band of the faithful; her visit to the tomb that first Easter morning and her vision of the risen Christ.

He found another by the name of Matthew sitting at the tax collector's bench; two others called James and John working on their father's fishing boat, and a man named Andrew brought him another named Simon, sur-named Peter. He almost caught another, an angry young rebel by the name of Judas, but a wave tore him out of his grasp at the last minute before he could draw him to safety. He was not too weary on the cross to see another even there.

There is a piece of driftwood on my bookcase; if it had a soul it might wish it could have been a piece of timber in a house, a part of a table, the arm of a chair, or any of a thousand useful things. We found the remains of a wooden wagon wheel not fifty feet from where we found that stump. What irony there was in that! Something that had seen so much service beside something so useless!

It would be rather easy to be cynical about driftwood if you think only of the wasted years; but there is more to be said than that. If you are young and uncommitted as you read this, I offer you the reminder a preacher gave to me some years ago. "Don't let your life end up as driftwood." But if it is too late for that advice, remember—God has made some beautiful things out of driftwood.

They that go down to the sea in ships, . . . these see the works of the Lord, and his wonders in the deep.

Psalm 107:23, 24 (KJV)

MEDITATION and WATER

Herman Melville once wrote, "Meditation and water are wedded forever." I know it has been true for me. The mountains were my first love and they will always be my greatest, but the sea runs them a close second.

I was twenty-five before I met the sea. I had seen the ocean before—even crossed it—but like many of life's experiences, I had never really met it. Then I spent a week on the New Jersey shore. I walked the beaches and listened to the slap of the waves on the sand; I awaited the relentless progress of the tide; from an island a few miles from the coast I watched the bay swallow the sun and watched the next morning as the sea reluctantly spewed it forth again; I saw the moonlight on the breakers as they rolled along the shore, and I fell in love with the sea.

Perhaps the secret of the ocean's fascination is that it sings an ancient song of origins that touches the chords of primeval memory buried within us. Some day space may replace the sea as the great symbol of mystery. A few thousand miles of ocean and a lifeboat can hardly compete with an astronaut and the immeasurable distances of space. And yet—when we seek words to describe such experiences, where do we turn? Back to the sea.

We speak of "the ocean of space" and "the sea of stars"; we call their craft a "ship"; the astronaut takes his walk in space "anchored" to the vessel with a "lifeline"; and when they complete their journey they come home again into the bosom of the sea. For most of us space travel will remain a vicarious experience, brought to us by men like McDivitt and White, through the courtesies of the detached description of Huntley and Brinkley. The sea will remain the mystery we can touch.

The main feeling the sea brings to me is that of awe and wonder that is akin to reverence. I suppose my respectable book of science could give me a factual explanation of the reasons for the tide and the ceaseless, endless beating of the waves upon the sand. I have read a bit about the tides, but somehow the explanation has not taken away the wonder of it all. The description was enlightening, but the experience was inspiring, and that has made the difference. My heart agrees with the psalmist who wrote, "They that go down to the sea, . . . these see the works of the Lord, and his wonders in the deep."

The other feeling I get when I go down to the sea is a little harder to describe. Call it a sense of something known and unknown, of something near yet far away, something immanent and transcendent. Here is the sea, lapping at my feet, yet it stretches for hundreds of miles, encompassing shores and islands and people of whom I have never seen or heard. What a lesson in the nearness and farness of God!

I do not believe there are as many people who have trouble believing in God as there are people who have difficulty in believing in a God who is personally interested in them. All our scientific knowledge simply pushes causes and origins back a bit farther. All our explorations into space only widen the horizons of the concept of God we have had for centuries. Our danger is not so much that we lose God as it is that we lose the personal contact with him.

"I can believe in God as Creator," I hear someone say. "I can believe in some Great Originator, some First Cause, some Primal Power; but what has that to do with me?" If you who read this feel that way, I suggest that you go down to the sea and ponder its nearness and its vastness. God is so great that we can think of him only in symbolic terms but he has a nearness that touches even the smallest island.

There are many wonders in the sea. These are only a few. Go down to the sea and listen for yourself.

ROADSIDE ALTARS

Take heed that you do not offer your burnt offerings at every place that you see.
Deuteronomy 12:13

One day last summer a friend and I were working on a new filmstrip depicting our Conference Camping Program. We had driven nearly two hundred miles one Sunday afternoon to get pictures of a canoe trip which a group of youth and their counselors were beginning. We wanted some general pictures around the campsite as well as some specific ones for which we would need to pose some of the young people. The pictures we planned to pose were the more important because they were needed to illustrate specific material in the script already written.

We arrived late in the afternoon, with not very much time left to get the lighting we needed for the pictures, so we both got busy taking shots around the camp and setting up some of the posed ones. We were so busy getting the pictures we wanted that no one bothered to keep track of how many pictures were being taken. We had plenty of film, or so we thought. There was one particular scene I wanted to include, of a camper reading a New Testament as they would do during the morning devotion period before they started on the river. I wanted it with a canoe and the river in the background. I drafted two campers to carry the canoe to a good spot and found another to sit for the picture. It was then that I noticed that I had only one exposure left on my last roll of film.

Since this was a necessary print for the script, I wanted to take two or three exposures so we could then pick the one that came out best. I called to my friend to take the picture, only to learn that all his film was used up. Here we were, two hundred miles from home, several miles from any location to purchase film, and no time left in the day to go after any even if we knew where to go.

It wasn't that we hadn't had enough film to start with; we had. It was simply that we became so interested in snapping anything that looked interesting that we neglected to keep in mind one of the pictures that was most necessary. Fortunately the one exposure turned out well; but it could just as easily have not. It is a dangerous thing to use so much material on what is interesting that there is little left for what is important.

How easy it is for life to become like that; burning itself out in so many interesting but trivial concerns that there is nothing left to give when something really vital comes along. How many lives have been wasted, not because they had nothing to offer, but because they poured out their offering at every roadside altar they came upon; and when they discovered the Shrine of shrines, they had nothing left to offer.

Many a man and woman have found what they thought was a good thing in life, a career, a club, an organization or several of them, or a special interest of one kind or another, and have given themselves to those interests with abandon. There may be nothing wrong in any of these in themselves, but often other matters are neglected in the process. One day they wake up and see the importance of their home and of communication and understanding with their companions and their children. How difficult they find it is to scrape together even a token offering after so many years of worshiping at roadside altars. "Take heed that you do not offer your burnt offerings at every place that you see."

A certain man had two sons; and he came to the first, and said, Son, go work to-day in my vineyard. He answered and said, I will not: but afterward he repented, and went. And he came to the second, and said likewise. And he answered and said, I go, sir: and went not.
Matthew 21:28-30 (KJV)

The wooded slopes across the lake had changed from shadowed detail to silhouette, and their mirrored reflection in the silent lake made one almost want to stand on his head to see which one was real. The weariness of the day had retreated with the sun, leaving behind it a quiet calmness that was content with the approaching darkness. In the wilderness, night has a chance to come leisurely; in the city, we just turn out the lights.

The sound of singing by the lake seemed most appropriate to the setting. It had changed from the boisterous, noisier songs to some of the more quiet ones in keeping with the mood around us. Earlier in the evening the mood of the singing had been quite different, switching back and forth between the semi-sacred and the unquestionably secular with such abandon that I found myself trying to decide whether we sing songs with our feet or with our minds. That evening I voted in favor of feet; it is the tunes and not the words that people are attracted to.

I don't say this critically; it is just that a switch from "Swing Low, Sweet Chariot" to "Waltzing Matilda" is more understandable when one is singing tunes than when one is considering words and meanings. Maybe I am looking for too neat an answer. Perhaps, like many things in life, it is not a matter of either/or but of both. Perhaps man seeks satisfaction to both mind and emotions and is simply willing to look for satisfaction of one interest one place and the other interest some place else. Perhaps he doesn't really care whether the words and the tune go together or not; and yet, I am haunted by the feeling that if that is the way things are, it shouldn't be.

As I thought about the matter, I wondered if this division I sensed in our approach to music was not a parable of life. Let the words be equated with what we know and say we ought to do, and let the tune equal what we feel and want to do, and are we not confronted with life's basic problem, that of getting the words and music to go together.

It is easy to conclude that it is better to do than to say. We have all known people who act better than they talk, and live better than they look; sort of hypocrites in reverse. On the other hand, who has not been acquainted with those who make loud and long profession concerning their intended actions, but who can't seem to find the melody to transform their words into a song of life? Furthermore, I doubt that any of us would hesitate very long in choosing between the two types as a neighbor or a friend. A harsh tongue and a big heart is far easier to take than a soft voice and a heart of stone.

The problem of not having the tune to go with the words is familiar enough, but the other aspect has its problems too. Haven't you had the frustrating experience of finding a tune stuck in your mind all day, whistling or humming it under your breath, but never quite being able to put the words to it and get it out? If someone asks you what the song is you're really in a fix, because all you have is the tune. It may be a grand tune, but it leaves you eternally unsatisfied because a man just as naturally yearns for words. Quite often, if one does not have the right words for the song, other words will be made up to accompany it which may not be worthy of the music that is being sung. If a few of the new words don't quite fit, it becomes an easy thing to mend the tune a little, and so the whole song becomes corrupted.

I often have the feeling that if the youths in some of the way-out movements today had heard a little more words *and* music from their elders, instead of just snatches of one or the other, they might have bought the whole song instead of wandering about whistling parts of an ancient melody and mumbling some great words without making much sense out of them.

The songs that really endure for more than a season or two are the ones that say something as well as sound good. The others come and go, but the ones that have words and music that go together keep coming back.

THORNS and THISTLES

Blessed is the man that endureth temptation: for when he is tried, he shall receive the crown of life.
James 1:12 (KJV)

I was in no mood to stop and philosophize when I came to the thorn thicket. I was hurrying to make it back to camp before dark, or at least to the old logging road that would get me there without the danger of falling and breaking a leg. The prospects of picking my way slowly through a thicket whose extent I didn't know, at the risk of clothing and skin, or of detouring around it were hardly faced in a detached manner. The thinking about it came later.

Why do we have such objectionable and uncomfortable things as thorns and thistles? I have run into them all my life. There were the thistles that used to pop up almost overnight in the pasture near the house where I liked to run barefooted as a boy; there were the rough lessons to learn about what

124

kind of trees you could and could not climb; there was some wood that, while it burned well, was not the easiest from which to whittle shavings.

Even more difficult to understand is why things so harmful have to appear so innocent, or even attractive. Some of the thistles have lovely blossoms; the locust tree is beautiful in bloom; the thorn tree looks easier than many other trees to climb. But woe to the unsuspecting who are deceived by appearances!

Later in life I learned that there are equally attractive but unpleasant experiences of far more consequence than stepping on a thistle in the field or picking up a dried locust branch. And yet I found points of similarity between some of life's unpleasant experiences, and thorns and thistles growing in our fields. In neither instance is it very obvious why we should have such things in our world. Like the thorns and thistles, they were often more attractive than they should have been, and both have to be dealt with whether we understand them or not.

Some people get so hung up on the "why" that they never get around to the "how" of living. Harry Emerson Fosdick once made the acute observation that Jesus never said he had explained the world; he said he had overcome it. This is not to say that we need make no effort to understand life, but it is to suggest that there is nothing about man that requires the universe to justify its existence to him. We have managed to replace the old theory that the sun revolves around the earth with one more akin to reality; but we are still obsessed with the inclination to interpret the world in terms of our own convenience.

We see a field of plants growing wild in the springtime and call them beautiful; we find some of the same in our lawn and spray them with weed killer. The rains come and bring new life to our gardens and refresh our streams and lakes and we call it good, but if these refreshing showers fall on a day we have planned an outing, we groan and complain about the weather. We read of tragic accidents in the newspaper and perhaps have a passing question about it, but when the same thing comes to us we often ask, "Why did this happen to me?" Have you ever pondered the implications of that question? It implies that we could understand it happening to someone else.

Perhaps the fact that the Christian faith makes so bold a claim to a personal relationship with God makes us prone to the idea that he should explain and justify all things to us. There is more than humor in the story of the minister who was traveling next to a very nervous lady in a transatlantic flight, when engine trouble developed in first one and then two of the four motors. The woman had been nervous before any trouble occurred; but as each engine coughed and sputtered and the plane pitched while the pilot trimmed its speed and balanced the engines, she became more and more agitated. The minister continued to read his book and perhaps had not noticed the trouble, but when the lady saw the exhaust from the third engine and mistook the sparks for flames she could stand it no longer.

127

Frantically she tugged at the pastor's sleeve and demanded, "We're going to crash! We're going to crash! You're a minister, do something." To which the minister replied, "I'm sorry, madam, but I'm in sales, not management." We are prone to forget that. We are prone to forget that there are sometimes things which are not explainable to a child, even when a father knows the answers. For all our vaunted wisdom, it is still conceivable that we have not yet learned all that there is to learn. Even the wisest man lives in abysmal ignorance when what he knows is compared with that which he does not know.

Fortunately, however, it is not always necessary for one to be able to explain something in order to know what to do with it. One does not have to have all the answers to live effective lives. One does not have to be able to explain why there are temptations in order to know that something has to be done about them. "Blessed is the man that endureth temptation."